ENVIRONMENTAL
ENGINEER

By Geoffrey M. Horn

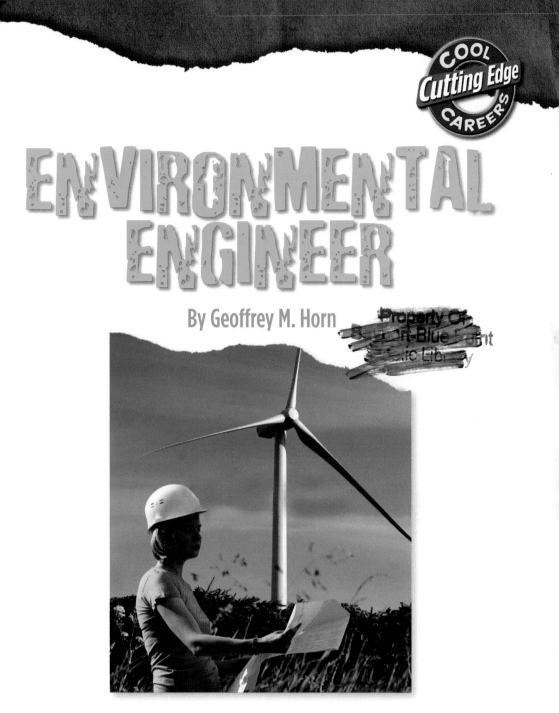

Content Adviser: Ezekiel Fugate, Yale University, Environmental Engineering Ph.D. Candidate

Gareth Stevens
Publishing

Please visit our web site at **www.garethstevens.com.**
For a free catalog describing Gareth Stevens Publishing's list of high-quality books,
call 1-800-542-2595 (USA) or 1-800-387-3178 (Canada).
Gareth Stevens Publishing's fax: 1-877-542-2596

Library of Congress Cataloging-in-Publication Data
Horn, Geoffrey M.
    Environmental engineer / by Geoffrey M. Horn.
        p. cm. — (Cool careers: cutting edge)
    Includes bibliographical references and index.
    ISBN-10: 1-4339-1956-7   ISBN-13: 978-1-4339-1956-5 (lib. bdg.)
    ISBN-10: 1-4339-2155-3   ISBN-13: 978-1-4339-2155-1 (soft cover)
    1. Environmental protection—Juvenile literature. 2. Sanitary engineers—Juvenile
literature. 3. Sanitary engineering—Juvenile literature. 4. Environmental
engineering—Juvenile literature. 5. Environmental engineers—Juvenile literature.
    I. Title.
TD170.15.H67 2010
628—dc22   2009004746

This edition first published in 2010 by
Gareth Stevens Publishing
A Weekly Reader® Company
1 Reader's Digest Rd.
Pleasantville, NY 10570-7000 USA

Executive Managing Editor: Lisa M. Herrington
Senior Editor: Brian Fitzgerald
Senior Designer: Keith Plechaty
Produced by Editorial Directions, Inc.
Art Direction and Page Production: Paula Jo Smith Design

Picture credits: Cover, title page, Andrei Merkulov/Shutterstock; p. 5 NASA; p. 6
Matt Stroshane/Getty Images; p. 9 Jupiter Images/Banana Stock/Alamy; p. 11 Robert
Nickelsbert/Getty Images; p. 13 Andrew Holbrooke/Corbis; p. 15 Karyn Mitchell; p. 17
Joseph Sohm/Visions of America/Corbis; p. 18 Peter Essick/Aurora/Getty Images; p. 19
Associated Press; p. 20 Gabe Palmer/Alamy; p. 21 Jeff Greenberg/Alamy; p. 23 Spencer
Platt/Getty Images; p. 24 Associated Press; p. 25 David Buimovitch/AFP/Getty Images;
p. 26–27 Image Source; p. 28 Anthony Dunn/Alamy

Printed in the United States of America

1 2 3 4 5 6 7 8 9 14 13 12 11 10 09

CONTENTS

Words in the glossary appear in **bold** type the first time they are used in the text.

CHAPTER 1
MEETING CHALLENGES

Getting a cool drink of water is easy when all you need to do is turn on the tap. But for astronauts living in the **International Space Station**, getting water to drink is no easy matter. In the past, a shuttle or cargo rocket carried water up into space. That was wasteful and expensive. For years, National Aeronautics and Space Administration (NASA) scientists searched for a better way.

In November 2008, NASA launched the space shuttle *Endeavour*. On board was a new piece of equipment for the space station. It is called a water recovery system. It's also called a space toilet. It can produce about 6,000 pounds (2,700 kilograms) of drinking water each year. How does it work? This cutting-edge system turns the astronauts' urine and sweat into clean, pure water.

Is this magic? No, it's just good, solid science. The **environmental engineers** at NASA had a problem to solve, and they solved it. Do you like solving problems and meeting challenges? Then environmental engineering may be the right career for you.

Endeavour lands after making a special delivery to the International Space Station in 2008.

What Does an Environmental Engineer Do?

Environmental engineers at NASA focus on what people need to live in space and on the Moon. Most environmental engineers work on more down-to-earth things. They find practical ways to protect the environment. They work to keep our water pure and our air clean. They protect our living spaces from dangerous chemicals and harmful waste.

On the Job:
NASA Project Manager

Bob Bagdigian works at the Marshall Space Flight Center in Huntsville, Alabama. He heads NASA's Environmental Control and Life Support System project. His team developed the water recovery system for the International Space Station.

He told a reporter for the Discovery Channel that his team had carried out taste tests with water from the new system. "Nobody had any strong objections," he said. "It tastes fine to me," he added. Bagdigian said that Marshall had first hired him in 1985. His current project? Planning life-support systems for a base on the Moon.

Bob Bagdigian explains his water recovery system.

Environmental engineers design and run systems that clean water and **sites** that dispose of trash. They look for ways to clean up polluted water, air, and land. They deal with accidents and emergencies that cause serious pollution problems.

Some of today's cutting-edge environmental engineers are focusing on how we design goods and services from the earliest stages. They believe that we can prevent pollution and other serious problems this way. They are also looking for new ways to use the Sun, wind, and water as energy sources.

Government and Private Firms

Engineers working for the government help draw up **regulations** to control pollution. Regulations are rules or laws that tell people what they can and can't do.

Engineers in private firms help companies understand and follow those rules. For example, national, state, and local governments have rules telling companies where and how they may drill for oil. Engineers help these firms use drilling methods that will do as little damage as possible. The best solutions do more than just protect the environment. They also save the companies money.

Many environmental engineers work for private companies. Some do all their work for one company. Others are **consultants**. These workers may offer advice to several different businesses.

Is Environmental Engineering the Right Job for You?

To find out whether you have the right stuff to be an environmental engineer, consider these questions:

- Do you enjoy helping the environment?
- Are you good at solving problems?
- Can you work well in an emergency?
- Do you like the outdoors?

Environmental engineers need a college degree in science or engineering. They often also earn one or more advanced degrees. Many colleges and universities offer special programs in environmental engineering. "Also study business," advises NASA engineer Cindy Upton. "You have to be able to track costs and understand where you need to spend the budget."

A Growing Field

The number of jobs in environmental engineering is expected to grow quickly. President Barack Obama has promised to spend more money on engineering projects. So the job picture may get even brighter.

After you get a job, you'll need to keep up with the latest developments. Governments and businesses are always looking for newer, better, and cheaper ways to control pollution.

What You Can Do Right Now

Here are some things you can do right now to help the environment:

- Encourage your family to walk, ride bikes, or use public transportation instead of driving.

- Turn off lights, TVs, radios, and other electrical things that you aren't using.

- Don't waste water. Ask your parents to fix leaky pipes and faucets.

- Recycle glass, paper, and plastic products. If your school doesn't have a recycling program, start one. Use rechargeable batteries.

- Put waste in trash cans, litter baskets, or recycling bins. Help your school organize a litter pick-up day.

- Don't smoke. If you know smokers, encourage them to stop.

- Think about the things you buy. Where do they go when you are finished with them? Choose products with less packaging. Use your own bags when you shop.

CHAPTER 2

PREVENTING POLLUTION

P ollution comes in many forms. An old bus or truck pollutes the air with smelly fumes. Hog and chicken farms can pollute streams with animal wastes. Factories can pollute the land with dangerous chemicals.

People pollute by littering. But using a trash can doesn't make the trash disappear. Cutting-edge environmental engineering works toward designing a world with less trash to throw away.

Pollution is not only ugly. It's also unhealthy. For example, polluted air can harm the eyes, nose, throat, and lungs. Air pollution is dangerous for people with breathing problems, such as asthma. In 1952, badly polluted air in London, England, killed 4,000 people in a few days.

Environmental engineers fight pollution in two ways. The first way is to stop pollution before it starts. This method is called prevention.

Coal smoke pours out of a
power plant in Pennsylvania.

Environmental engineers also fight pollution by cleaning up polluted sites. This method is called **remediation**. The term comes from the word *remedy*, which means "cure." The United States spends billions of dollars on remediation every year. Preventing pollution is almost always cheaper and better.

Planning Pays Off

The United States has many laws to prevent pollution. There is the Clean Air Act of 1970, the Clean Water Act of 1972, and the Safe Drinking Water Act of 1974. Environmental engineers help companies obey these laws.

Another important law is the National Environmental Policy Act. This law took effect in 1970. It requires the U.S. government to consider the environment when planning a new project. A major project like an airport or a superhighway can cause tremendous damage if not properly planned.

The U.S. government controls a lot of land. Companies that want to build, dig, or drill on this land need a **permit**. To get a permit, companies submit plans telling the government how their projects will affect the environment. Companies count on environmental engineers to prepare these plans.

To protect the environment, the government may require builders to change their plans. Environmental engineers must then carry out these changes. The project should cause the least possible damage to the environment. Environmental engineers must be involved in planning a project from beginning to end, not just in the early stages.

An EPA scientist examines waste water from a treatment plant.

EPA Jobs and Training Programs

Some environmental engineers work at the Environmental Protection Agency (EPA). It's part of the U.S. government. The EPA started in 1970. It employs about 17,000 people. Many of them are environmental engineers and scientists.

The EPA runs several career-training programs. The Student Career Experience Program (SCEP) and Student Temporary Employment Program (STEP) are aimed at high school and college students. You must be at least 16 years old to enter these programs. Other programs help college students who want to do research on the environment.

Improving Air Quality

Air quality in the United States is a great success story. Since Congress passed the Clean Air Act, the nation's air has gotten much better. Special control devices called scrubbers in factory smokestacks prevent pollution from entering the air. Devices attached to car and truck engines trap harmful gases before they can escape. A shift from coal to cleaner-burning fuels like natural gas has helped. So have efforts to convince Americans not to smoke cigarettes.

Environmental engineers write, enforce, and help companies follow the rules that make our air cleaner. Scientists recently studied the effects of cleaner air in 51 major U.S. city centers. The experts found that improved air quality helped people live longer.

Serious Challenges

Some countries still have very serious air pollution problems. China gets much of its power from coal. Burning coal pollutes the air and covers buildings with dust.

Factories in China, which make many of the products that Americans buy, are also major polluters. Air-quality standards there are poor. Environmental engineers in China face some of the toughest challenges in the world today.

On the Job: Environmental Engineer Jessica Dooling

Jessica Dooling works for a natural-gas production company in Colorado. Her job site is in the Piceance Basin, one of the world's newest natural-gas drilling areas.

Q: When did you become interested in environmental science?

Dooling: I absolutely hated science in high school. But I had some interest in environmental issues. I went to Brookdale Community College in New Jersey. A professor there suggested environmental science as a career. I got my bachelor's degree from Rutgers University in New Jersey.

Q: What challenges do you face in your current job?

Dooling: We have to deal with some of the most **restrictive** drilling rules in the United States. One of the biggest issues is waste disposal. Regulations are much stricter than 20 years ago. The cost to the company is incredible. We truck some of the waste to other states for disposal. If we can reduce the amount of waste, that can mean a huge cost savings to the company.

Q: What do you like most about your job?

Dooling: The thing I like about environmental science the most is that it's constantly changing. You don't need to be a math whiz. You don't need to be a science whiz. You just need to apply yourself.

CHAPTER 3

HAZARDOUS MATERIALS

Homes in the United States produce more than 250 million tons of garbage each year. This giant mountain of trash includes food scraps, food packages, grass clippings, glass bottles, metal cans, plastics, and other materials. About one-third of the trash is recycled or turned into **compost**. Trucks take the rest to dumps and **landfills**. Some environmental engineers earn their living designing and managing landfills.

Some materials are too dangerous to handle this way. They are called hazardous materials, or **hazmats**. Dealing with hazmats is a major problem for environmental engineers everywhere.

Types of Hazards

The U.S. government lists more than 500 kinds of hazmats. Each poses a risk to human health. The government has outlawed some of these materials.

Other hazmats are in many of the things we use every day, such as paint, car batteries, motor

CAUTION
HAZARDOUS WASTE SITE
DIOXIN CONTAMINATION
• STAY IN YOUR CAR
• MINIMIZE TRAVEL
• KEEP WINDOWS CLOSED •
• STAY ON PAVEMENT
• DRIVE SLOWLY
USEPA, KANSAS CITY (816) 374-6529

This sign warns drivers about a dangerous chemical called dioxin.

oil, and computer parts. They are safe when used and stored correctly. People can't just dump them anywhere, however. They must get rid of hazmats properly. Find out about local drop-off sites from your town or city.

Medical waste also causes a problem. Needles and anything else that comes in contact with blood can carry disease. Medical waste needs to be treated with great care. It must be burned or **disinfected** before it goes in a landfill.

Nuclear waste is another huge problem. Electric power plants that use nuclear fuel produce this waste.

Making nuclear bombs also produces this kind of waste. Nuclear waste is very dangerous and lasts a very long time. Environmental engineers are working hard to find safe ways to store it.

Cleaning Up

In the past, thousands and thousands of sites in the United States became seriously polluted. Companies had stored or dumped poisonous chemicals incorrectly.

An engineer uses remote controls to move nuclear waste between tanks.

Environmental engineers help clean up oil spills.

On the Job: Oil Spill Expert

Dr. Roy W. Hann Jr. is a professor at Texas A&M University. He has worked as both a teacher and a consultant. He studied engineering at the University of Oklahoma. Later, he headed the environmental engineering program at Texas A&M. He is one of the world's top experts on cleaning up oil spills. "The environmental engineering field is here to stay," he says. "The oil spill and hazardous material field will be important as long as we use oil and manufacture hazardous material." Hann believes that prevention is the best approach.

Cleaning With SOUL

Not all cleanup jobs require high-tech solutions. In the mid-1990s, the Save Our Urban Land (SOUL) program began to turn trash-filled lots in Chicago, Illinois, into beautiful gardens. In this award-winning effort, teens helped clean up garbage, scrap metals, and other junk. They improved the land. They also got rid of a major source of water pollution. The program gave teens a hands-on opportunity to explore careers in environmental science.

Many cleanup crews, including this one in Miami, Florida, improve U.S. cities.

The poisons seeped into the soil and into the water supply. Sometimes this happened by accident. In other cases, companies broke the law. When some of those firms went out of business, there was no money left to clean up the sites.

The U.S. government set up a program to clean up polluted sites in 1980. This program is called the **Superfund**. Environmental engineers work with other specialists to find and study polluted sites. They use Superfund money to clean them up. This work is

Superfund sites require protective clothing. This worker measures polluted soil.

slow and difficult. Polluted soil can't just be dumped somewhere else. Engineers use advanced science and creative ideas to make these sites safe for people to use.

CHAPTER 4

WATER, WATER EVERYWHERE

E ngineers are building one of the largest water projects in the world underneath New York City. Few people will ever see New York City Water Tunnel Number 3, but the work is cutting edge. The project will not be finished until at least 2020.

The tunnel will carry water about 60 miles (95 kilometers), from upstate New York to more than 8 million people who live in the city. The cost? At least $6 billion. When this tunnel is finished, engineers must face another challenging project. New York City Water Tunnel Number 1, opened in 1917, needs repairs badly.

Serving a Thirsty World

New York isn't the only U.S. city with water problems. In 2009, the American Society of Civil Engineers (ASCE) issued a report card on the country's water and other basic systems.

The ASCE gave the nation's water systems a grade of D minus. It said leaky pipes lose about 7 billion

New York City's new Water Tunnel Number 3 will carry fresh, clean water to millions of people.

gallons (26 billion liters) of clean drinking water every day. Environmental engineers will need to repair and improve these systems.

The challenges in other parts of the world are even greater. About 1.1 billion people lack safe, clean water. More than twice that number do not have modern toilets and **sewage** systems. Raw, untreated sewage can pollute rivers and spread disease. In much of the world, raw sewage is a very serious environmental problem.

Clean Water Saves Lives

Environmental engineers are concerned about clean water. You can turn on a faucet almost anywhere in a developed country and get clean, safe water. Water-related illnesses in developing countries are still a huge problem, however. In southern Africa's Zimbabwe, unclean water caused a major outbreak of cholera in 2008. Cholera is a very serious disease that can cause death. The World Health Organization (WHO) has reported more than 80,000 cases of cholera in Zimbabwe. More than 3,700 people have died from the disease.

Without a source for clean, safe water, many people in Zimbabwe use rainwater from city drains.

Old Challenges, New Methods

Environmental engineers have been dealing with water problems for a long time. Today, they are developing new ways to treat water and waste. They are also working to prevent pollution, control floods, and get water to farmers who need it.

Engineers in Saudi Arabia have made great progress in the Middle East. Much of the land there is desert, and freshwater is scarce. Engineers have figured out how to take the salt out of seawater and turn it into freshwater. This method is called **desalination**.

Today, Saudi Arabia has more than two dozen desalination plants. They supply drinking water to more than two-thirds of the country's people. Another country in the Middle East, Israel, gets much of its water from desalination.

CHAPTER 5

SAVING OUR EARTH

Environmental engineers can save lives by keeping our air and water clean. They can save money by helping companies find cheaper ways to prevent pollution. Now, they are being asked to help save our planet from a serious threat. That's **global warming**.

What Causes Global Warming?

The world gets most of its energy from fuels such as coal, oil, and natural gas. All these fuels contain carbon. When they burn, some of the carbon joins with the oxygen in the air. This produces a gas called **carbon dioxide**.

Carbon dioxide is a normal part of nature. In fact, trees and other green plants can't live without it. But when

Cars, trucks, and taxis contribute to city pollution.

we burn too much coal, oil, and gas, we produce too much carbon dioxide. When carbon dioxide and certain other gases fill the air, they trap some of the heat that Earth gets from the Sun. This makes our planet warmer.

Scientists believe that global warming damages the environment and threatens human life. The polar ice caps are already melting. This will make the oceans rise. As a result, some places in the world will have floods and other disasters. Diseases that thrive in warm weather may spread to new places.

How Can We Stop It?

Right now, engineers are working to find ways to stop global warming. They are developing ways to get energy from the wind and the Sun. China and the United States have huge amounts of coal. Research into "clean coal" may help find ways to burn coal without sending harmful gases into the air.

Cars that run on gasoline are another source of global warming. One of President Obama's first acts in office was to tighten rules on cars and trucks. Future cars and trucks must use less fuel and release fewer harmful gases. Automakers will need to work closely with environmental engineers to build new cars and engines that will help slow global warming.

Environmental engineers have much work to do. Their job is to meet the needs of today without damaging our ability to meet the needs of the future. If you're interested in meeting that challenge, environmental engineering might be the career for you.

Wind is a promising power source. These wind turbines produce energy in California.

Career Fact File

OUTLOOK

- About 54,000 Americans hold jobs as environmental engineers. More than 90,000 others work in related areas of environmental science.

- Environmental engineering is a rapidly growing field. Between 2006 and 2016, the number of jobs is expected to increase by 25 percent. More money from the U.S. government may make the job picture even better.

WHAT YOU'LL DO

- Many environmental engineers work to prevent, control, and reduce air and water pollution. Some help to protect the public from hazardous wastes.

- Environmental engineers seek creative, cutting-edge solutions to some of the world's most serious problems. They are developing ways to deal with global warming and to use water and energy more wisely.

- Some environmental engineers work for federal, state, and local governments. Others help private companies follow government rules and regulations.

WHAT YOU'LL NEED

- A solid background in math and science is key. Almost all engineering jobs require at least a college degree. Many environmental engineers also earn advanced degrees. Research and teaching positions often require a doctoral degree, or Ph.D.

- A love for the environment and the outdoors is important.

- Strong problem-solving skills are essential.

WHAT YOU'LL EARN

- Environmental engineers earn about $70,000 a year. Engineers who are at the top of their field may earn $100,000 or more.

Source: U.S. Department of Labor, Bureau of Labor Statistics

GLOSSARY

carbon dioxide — a colorless, odorless gas made of carbon and oxygen; it is produced when animals breathe and when fuel containing carbon burns

compost — a combination of plant and animal wastes used to fertilize farms and gardens

consultants — people who are paid to advise others

desalination — a method for removing salt from seawater

disinfected — treated in a way that destroys or prevents disease

environmental engineers — people who are trained to find safe ways to get rid of trash, turn waste water into clean water, control pollution, and protect our living spaces from hazardous materials

global warming — the slow rise in worldwide temperatures

hazmats — short for *hazardous materials*; poisons and other harmful substances

International Space Station — a large structure in space in which astronauts live and conduct experiments

landfills — places where trash is buried and covered with layers of dirt

permit — a written statement giving someone permission to do something

regulations — rules or laws that tell people what they can and can't do

remediation — the process of stopping or reversing environmental damage

restrictive — limiting

sewage — liquid and solid wastes produced by humans

sites — locations

Superfund — a U.S. government program to clean up sites polluted by dangerous chemicals

TO FIND OUT MORE

Books

David, Laurie, and Cambria Gordon. *The Down-to-Earth Guide to Global Warming.* New York: Orchard Books, 2007.

Ferguson Publishing. *Discovering Careers for Your Future: Environment.* New York: Ferguson Publishing, 2008.

Hall, Julie. *A Hot Planet Needs Cool Kids: Understanding Climate Change and What You Can Do About It.* Bainbridge Island, WA: Green Goat Books, 2007.

Rodger, Ellen. *Building a Green Community.* New York: Crabtree Publishing, 2008.

Web Sites

EEK! Get a Job

www.dnr.state.wi.us/org/caer/ce/eek/job/index.htm
Check out the Career Zones section of Environmental Education for Kids! site, created by the Wisconsin Department of Natural Resources.

EPA Climate Change Kids Site

www.epa.gov/climatechange/kids/index.html
Learn what you can do to fight global warming.

EPA Student Center

www.epa.gov/region5/students/
Check out fun activities and environmental club projects.

HowStuffWorks: Green Science Library

science.howstuffworks.com/green-science-channel.htm
Read detailed articles, see diagrams, and view videos showing the basic ideas behind environmental science.

Publisher's note to educators and parents: Our editors have carefully reviewed these web sites to ensure that they are suitable for children. Many web sites change frequently, however, and we cannot guarantee that a site's future contents will continue to meet our high standards of quality and educational value. Be advised that children should be closely supervised whenever they access the Internet.

INDEX

About the Author

Geoffrey M. Horn has written more than four dozen books for young people and adults, along with hundreds of articles for encyclopedias and other works. He lives in southwestern Virginia, in the foothills of the Blue Ridge Mountains, with his wife, their collie, and six cats. He dedicates this book to Jane Eigenrauch.